MW01206058

Beautifully Rational
Philosophy of
Astrology

By
Vic DiCara

Cover Photo: Bhanu DiCara

ISBN: **1514299275**

ISBN-13: **978-1514299272**

गौराब्दे ऋषियुग्वाणौ माघे श्रीमन्दिरानतरे ।
कूजाहे ऽसितपञ्चम्याम ग्रन्थो ऽयं पूर्णतां गतः ॥

gaurābde ṛṣi-yug-vāṇau
māghe śrī-mandirāntare
kūjāhe 'sita-pañcamyām
grantho 'yaṁ pūrṇatāṁ gataḥ

In golden years numbering
cupids arrows,
the divine couple,
and the sages,
During Māgha, in Śrī's temple,
On Tuesday,
when the moon waned five days,
This book attained completion.

(The predawn of January 21st, 2014)

PART 3 DIVINATION

Introduction

The Beautifully Rational Philosophy of Astrology explains the all-important ideological underpinnings of astrology and thus establishes its ongoing relevance and validity in the modern world.

Although this book is about the philosophy and rational basis of astrology, it is also practical; perhaps more than any how-to guide. After all, what could be more practical than knowledge?

Practicing anything with technical know-how but without philosophical comprehension is worse than impractical - it's *dangerous*. If I know how to work a saw, but don't know why and when a saw should be used... do you think the story will end well? I'll wind up buzzing walls, mauling furniture, chopping down crops, and worse (cue the theme music from Texas Chainsaw Massacre). The most practical knowledge is *why* to use a thing. Only then is it truly useful to know *how* to use that thing.

This book will not leap into paint-by-the-number technical recipes for answering specific questions typically posed to an astrologer. It will instead answer the most fundamentally practical questions, like: Does astrology work? If so, why? When should we resort to astrology, and when shouldn't we? What is really to gain from astrology?

This book doesn't give recipes for answering specific questions, but it creates a foundation on which you can answer *all* questions.

Part 1
The Rationale of Astrology

Chapter One:

The Genesis of Astrology

It's hard for even the most starry-eyed astrology fan not to notice that when most modern people hear the word *astrology* they envision images of hoodoo-voodoo-ism. In all honesty, right from the get-go I should admit that they're a little bit *right*. Maybe 90% of the "astrology" floating around out there these days is painfully bogus stuff that would be lucky to qualify as bona-fide voodoo. Nonetheless in my opinion astrology is not *intrinsically* an outright hoax, even if so much of it today is so hokey. At the very least it's a fact that the foundations of astrology are the foundations of our revered modern sciences. Astrology - the original, core form of it - is the mother of all science and technology, although this can be a deceptive statement if we don't define what the "original, core form" of astrology actually is.

The original core of astrology is not fortune-telling, it's the science of telling time.

Telling time is a really important skill because if you can't tell the time you die pretty quick. If you don't know the time of day you don't know when it's going to get dark, which means you won't know how much time you have left before you need to be safe indoors, and so on. It's probably even more important to be able to tell the time of year. If you don't you won't be able to prepare for winter, and you'll pretty likely freeze to death or starve.

The science of telling time is humanity's first science because it generates the technology required to solve humanity's first and most immediate problem: survival.

The Science of Telling Time

These days we just look at our cell phones or wristwatch and that's that - we know what time it is. The ease with which we now tell time is a luxury enjoyed as a result of centuries of science and technology built upon the core of astrology.

Maybe it's hard to immediately see the connection between astrology and telling time, but if we didn't have our cell phones, wristwatches and so on we'd suddenly understand the connection really well. Imagine yourself dropped on an island in the middle of a world without calendars, clocks, computers, cell-phones or any of that stuff. How would you figure out what time it was?

Sunrise and sunset would be awfully important, wouldn't they?

You could, for example, mark the beginning of a *day* with each sunrise. And you could get more refined by measuring how far the sun has progressed from sunrise towards sunset. This would enable you to keep track of *hours* and know in advance when the darkness is coming.

So we begin to notice that time is based on the movement of the sun. We begin to realize that time has to do with the movement of celestial bodies.

How can you keep track of hours at night? The moon. When the sun goes down, the moon comes up. Or does it? On closer inspection, sometimes it does, but sometimes it doesn't.

"Closer inspection," by the way, is the mother of empirical observation, the essential skill required for any science.

The moon has a more complicated pattern of rising and setting, connected with its changing shape. When the moon is perfectly round, it will rise as the sun sets and spend the whole night illuminating the starry sky. With each sunrise thereafter the Moon becomes less round and rises later and later, leaving more and more of the early night bereft of illumination. After eight sunrises (eight "days") the moon won't rise until midnight, and when it does it will be only half round! After 15 sunrises the moon will have waned past the thinnest crescent, completely disappeared, and won't rise at all!

That's a little bit alarming, but thankfully the world doesn't end. Two or three days later, in the very early evening, you'll find a crescent sliver of moon just above the western horizon, shining with only a fraction of her light on just a fraction of the early evening. Every day thereafter, she'll get more round and stays out a bit longer. Eight days later she's grown to half-round, rises at noon and becomes visible in the blue sky as the sun dims towards the afternoon, staying out past sunset to illuminate the entire first half of the night before setting at midnight. After fifteen days of growth she'll again be fully round, rise exactly when the sun sets, and illuminate the entire night.

The need for observations like these generated the initial empirical skills that eventually evolved into the foundations of our modern sciences. That's why astrology is legitimately described as the mother of science, the original science.

Awareness of the moon's cycle not only grants you knowledge of the hours at night, it also lets you keep track of *fortnights* (fifteen days of "brightening" nights as the moon waxes, and fifteen days of "darkening" nights as she wanes). It also lets you measure *months*. Did you notice how long it takes the Moon to complete a whole cycle from fully round to totally empty and back again? Fifteen days from full to empty and fifteen days to get back again to full – thirty days: a month.

So, just by watching the sun and moon, you could keep track of hours, days, fortnights, and months even if you were in a primeval wilderness without any modern aids. That would make you more than just an attractive nerd - it would make you better equipped to *survive*, and would put you well on your way to attaining the goal of science: making sense of the world you live in.

What's a Year?

Still, you're probably going to die out there unless you can figure out how to keep track of your position in an even more important unit of time: a year.

The seasons let us know that the year is coming and going, and we would notice right away that there are very close to 12 full-moons (months) in a year. It would be after a few years that the "very close" part would start to make a difference. The moon makes a bit *more* than 12 cycles in a year. In a few years this starts to throw the seasons out of whack with our primitive calendars. After a while we would wind up trying to plant and harvest at increasingly inopportune times.

So we discovered two better ways to measure the year: by starlight, or by sunlight.

How to Measure a Year by Starlight.

This one is a little difficult. You'll need to wake up a little before sunrise every day, because you have to keep track of the sun's position relative to the stars, and the moments just before dawn are the closest we can get to seeing the stars and the sun at the same time. Wake up just before dawn and look carefully at the sky just above the eastern horizon, just before the dawn becomes too bright and the blue sky hides the stars.

Make a sketch of it. Do this for a month or two and compare your predawn sky sketches. You'll find that they gradually change - the stars gradually move in relation to the sunrise!

As you keep sketching, week after week your sketches will keep changing significantly, until one day you will make a sketch that is exactly the same as the first one you made 365 sunrises ago.

Exactly one "year" will have passed.

That's how you measure a year by starlight: watch the predawn sky and wait for the sun to return to a reference-star.

There are two problems with this method: (1) It's not the easiest thing to do, and (2) its better than a 12-moon approximation, but its still not completely accurate. There's another way to measure a year that is easier and more accurate...

How to Measure a Year by Sunlight

For this, you can sleep till noon. Just take a tall, straight stick and plant it into the ground firmly at a right angle. Everyday at midday measure the length of the shadow it casts. You'll notice that the midday shadow will grow longer day by day, to a point, after which it shrinks day by day. The cool thing is that the shortest shadow of the year accurately marks the beginning of winter, and the longest shadow accurately marks the beginning of summer.

With nothing but a stick, you can accurately track the seasons and the passage of years. With this knowledge, humanity could more easily survive and thrive.

The First Astrological Charts

The core of astrology is the science of telling time. Thus the original astrological charts weren't "birth charts," they were calendars – drawing twelve months to a year, thirty days to a month, fifteen days to a fortnight, seven days to a week, and twenty-four hours to a day.

Why twenty-four hours in a day? Astrologers divided the day into 12 segments to reflect the twelve divisions of a year. Dividing the night in the same manner, we get 24 hours between one sunrise and the next.

Why are there seven days in a week? Well, two reasons: (1) it's the closest you can get to dividing a fortnight in half, and thus dividing a month into quarters; and (2) There are seven astrological planets. The Sun owns Sunday. The Moon owns Monday. Mars owns Tuesday (*Dies Martis* - "Day of Mars" - in Latin). Mercury owns Wednesday (*Dies Mercuri* - "Day of Mercury"). Jupiter owns Thursday (*Dies Jovis* - "Day of Jupiter"). Venus owns Friday (*Dies Veneris* - "Day of Venus"). Saturn, obviously, owns Saturday.

Why do the days, months and years start and end when they do?

These days, we start a new day at midnight. This is for the sake of having the date change while most people are asleep. Natural astrological days, however, start with the Sunrise.

Months start when the Moon reaches an obvious marker, usually a full Moon (since you can't exactly see the empty Moon). Or you can abstract that principle into a 12-fold ecliptic and start the month when the Sun enters a new twelfth. This is more like our modern system, but somehow our modern calendar months are consistently 10 or 11 days out of sync with the ecliptic divisions.

There are a few ways to determine the start of a year. One way starts the year on the first day of spring, because that's the day the Sun completes the final twelfth of its circuit. Another approach is to say that the shortest (or longest) day of the year marks the beginning of a new one. Our modern calendar starts on January 1st, which is just about 11 days later than the shortest day. Using the shortest day as the year's marker is very reasonable because it's the day on which the Sun starts "rising." As the sun rising over the horizon marks the beginning of a day, the sun rising from the nadir of its journey south of the equator is a good way to mark the beginning of a year.

By deciding all these conventions, astrologers created humanity's first astrological charts: calendars, and thus began to play a role they still play to this day: giving guidelines by which people can more fruitfully live their lives.

Chapter Two:

Tell the Time, Know the Future

Yes, astrology was originally more about time-telling than fortune-telling, but the really interesting thing is that there's very little difference between telling time and telling the future.

Knowing the time tells us about the present, but by knowing about the present we also gain knowledge of the past and future. For example, right now it's June 8th. By knowing this I also know that in a few weeks the summer is really going to kick in, and I know that just a weeks ago it became warm enough to keep my windows open at night.

Predicting a Broken Window

Knowledge of the current time reveals information about the past and the future, because past, present, and future are three aspects of a single entity.

To illustrate this, imagine some kids playing baseball in a vacant lot. One kid swings the bat and the ball flies off at a specific speed, in a specific direction.

Freeze that moment. It is a description of the present, yet embedded in it are details about the past and future.

By seeing the ball in mid air you can calculate the past (the ball leaving the pitcher's hand, the bat hitting the ball, etc.). Similarly, you can know the future, too. Calculating the direction and speed of the ball, you can foresee it crashing through a kitchen window, and probably the kids subsequently scattering like ants to hide from the doom of getting in lots of trouble.

Know any phase of time, and you can infer the other two, if you're smart and thorough. This is because past, present and future are three angles on the same thing: time. We usually think of the three phases of time as disjointed and different from one another, but they are *one* thing seen from three different vantage points. Since past, present and future are merely three windows on the same entity, it is theoretically rational that by knowing one of them you gain some access to all of them.

As the baseball example illustrates, the present inherently contains within it information about the past and future. Similarly each phase of time contains within it references to the other two phases. The more clearly you know one point in time, the more accurately you can calculate what the other points are like.

Let's go back to our baseball example. If, at any given moment, you precisely know the velocity and direction of the ball (and a zillion other minor variables like wind speed and so on), you can compute almost exactly which kid threw or hit it, and almost exactly where it's going to land. The more details you know about one point in the sequence of event, the more details you can extrapolate about the other points. Theoretically, if you know enough details, clearly enough, and are sufficiently expert in extrapolation, you can predict and postdict in amazing detail.

Now, remember that we use the position of the sun and moon to tell the current time. So its plausible that the position of the sun, moon and other luminaries might gives us

20

information about a point in time that we could use to extrapolate information about other points in time.

The theory rides on a proposal that the positions of objects in the heavens express information about moments in time through the symbolism of natural metaphors, beginning with the fundamental metaphor that the sun rising in the east symbolizes beginnings, and setting in the west symbolizes endings. An astrologer tallies the symbolic implications of all the heavenly lights at a given moment for a given place, and interprets their symbolism to understand the moment in time and space. Extrapolating upon that, the astrologer could divine implications on the present, past and future.

We Know a Little, Can We Know it All?

No one can deny that this theory works, at least for certain things like the sunrise, seasonal changes, and so on. But, does it work for more complex things like finding out if your ex-boyfriend will come back to you? It's tantalizing to think that it might. After all, we can foretell changes in the seasons, why shouldn't we be able to elaborate on that system and get even *more* knowledge about the future? Astrology can pretty easily predict exactly when the next sunrise will happen, so maybe it can also predict the next eclipse? Impressively enough, it can. So maybe it can also predict the daily weather, the outcome of a war, or even when John Doe will get a promotion at work?

"Observation of the sun and moon grants us some knowledge of the future," we say, "so maybe we can know *more* about the future if we observe the heavens in *more* detail. If we could observe everything about the motions of the heavens in absolute detail, maybe we could know *everything* about the past, present and future!?"

Ptolemy, the great mathematician, geographer, poet and founding forefather of classical astrology in Greece expressed this hypothesis in the second chapter of the first book of Tetrabiblos:

> *"If our heavenly observations and measurements were infinitely precise; if the symbolism we assigned to the heavens was infinitely perfect and relevant; if our interpretive intellect was infinitely subtle; and if our practical experience was infinitely vast... perhaps then we could predict the affairs of a human individual with 100% accuracy."*

The hypothesis is certainly thrilling, and not inherently unreasonable. The immediate problem, however, is the degree of thoroughness required to answer the types of questions most people are hopeful of having a fortune-teller answer for them. Such thoroughness involves observational and symbolic complexities that instantly expand beyond the limits of conventional human intelligence. Looking at the sun and moon and extrapolating the basic weather trend for the current season is one thing, and yes, it's quite impressive and complex, but imagine the incredible degree of sophistication and complexity required to extrapolate so extensively that you could, by observing the heavens, know when a specific human being at a specific point in history will get a promotion at work!

There's another problem with the theory, perhaps an even bigger hurdle. It assumes that exact details about the future are set and laid out as neat and orderly as the seasons and sunrises. What if they're not? What if the universe doesn't really care all that much of John Doe gets a promotion at work? What if our promotions and demotions aren't super important in the universal scheme and scale of things - and therefore aren't set in stone and preset into the universal hardwiring? If that's the case, than no matter how minutely we measure the heavens we'll never be able to answer John Doe's employment question in a concrete way, since that detail of the future doesn't even *exist* in a concrete way until it manifests in the present.

Considering these two hurdles it's no surprise that we who have practiced astrology with all our brain cells firing at full throttle have found a wall out there that we can't surmount. There's a limit to how much detail we can know about the future. When we try to push past that wall the complexity of the symbolic connections rapidly becomes astounding and short-circuits the human brain. There are simply *too many potentially valid interpretations* to sort through and assess.

Nonetheless my honest opinion is that there *really is* an uncanny symbolic connection between the positions of the heavens and the unfolding of an individual's destiny, and that this connection becomes relatively clear to a sincere astrologer with more frequency than odds would expect. Yes, there are significant limits to how well we can demystify that connection, but I think the fact that we can know anything at all is pretty amazing and exciting. We can't be all-knowing but there is a lot we *can* see about the future, past and so on. And, best of all, in my experience the things we can clearly see turn out to be the things we really need to see the most.

Wild Claims of Accuracy

Of course there is no shortage of (over-)confident astrologers who advertise and pose like they can scale the wall and know everything about anything whenever they want to. That's good old-fashioned *marketing,* folks. There's a whole lot of salesmen out there overestimating themselves and underestimating the complexity of the science, and, unfortunately, it sells relatively well to the uneducated masses, keeping the true science of astrology in severe remission.

The astrological community, perhaps especially in the "Vedic" hemisphere, is flooded by so many bold proclamations of predictions that are 80%, 90%, even 100% accurate. Let's take them to task, shall we?

I'm not a trained statistician but here's the basic outline of an experiment about claims of predictive accuracy.

Take a common, real world question, like, "When will I get married?" Think about how many possible answers there are to this question. There are 12 months in a year, and people are generally of marriageable age for 20 or more years. So, just to answer roughly to the month involves selecting from more than 240 possible answers. And then there's the probability that someone won't even get married at all - which is rising fast and in the US is now about half the adult population. A random guess therefore has about 0.4% of 50% chance of being right. In other words, a guess would be right 0.2% of the time. If someone could give the correct answer even 1% of the time, it means he or she sees the future four or five times more clearly than a random guess. If they can give the answer correctly just 10% of the time, it means they see the future forty or fifty times more clearly than chance would allow.

Just 10% accuracy is *forty or fifty times* more accurate than a normal guess!

Of course we don't have to make a random guess - we could make an educated guess. Let's say our querents are all US residents, all contemporary people, and all women. We can find out from the Internet that the average age for marriage among US women is now 27, and that weddings are very rarely held between November and March, so we could narrow our guess to the seven popular months and the most common age. Still how accurate will our educated guess be? It takes a real statistician to figure that out but here's a rough guesstimate:

First we have to be right that the person will get married at all. Since about half of our sample group never get married, we'll guess wrong about half the time we predict any marriage date.

Now we have to factor in the year. We're going to guess that marriage will happen in the 27th year, because this is the most popular age. I couldn't find out how popular. Is it half the female population who marries at 27 years old? I doubt it's that much. A quarter? That still seems awfully high, but to err on the side of caution, lets say a quarter of our sample of the female population get married at 27, if they marry at all. So if we make an educated guess that the lady on the other side of our crystal ball will marry when she is 27 years old, we'll be right 25% of 50% of the time. In other words, we'll 12.5% "accurate."

But, now we have to give the month. We're ruling out November through March, leaving seven possible months to guess from. Even if absolutely no one ever got married between November and March, we would still only guess right one out of seven times. That's 14.2% of 25% of 50%. In other words, an educated, intelligent guess has, on the very generous side, about 1.7% chance of being right.

If an astrologer could sustain even 10% accuracy over a large sample of individuals, that would demonstrate almost six times more clarity of future-vision than intelligence alone permits. Don't you think that's very significant? If your eyes were six times better than mine, do you know how helpful you would be to me as a guide?

If an astrologer could sustain 20% accuracy over a large sample, that would be amazing, wouldn't it?

But *lots* of astrologers are advertising 80, 90 and 100 percent accuracy. Now that we've looked at a real world example, maybe you have a sense of how audaciously bold those claims are. Obviously some wordplay and outright deception is going into those figures!

Anyway, try putting an honest sign above your fortune-telling booth saying "10%-20% Accuracy!" Not a whole lot of people are going to sit in front of your crystal ball. The crowds will form around the booths with neon signs flashing "100% Accuracy." The crowds just don't seem smart enough or skeptical enough to realize that it has to be false advertising. Even without knowing astrology or statistics, if anyone just thinks about it for a second they would figure out that if Joe Swami really had 100%, 90%, or even 70% perfect knowledge of the future he'd be living in the white house or better, not sitting behind a ball in a cheap corner of the mall or in the converted porch of a tiny old house, trying to figure out how to pay the bills while eating store-bought sandwiches. All the governments, stock traders, and major corporations of the world would be lined up to pile money at his feet for a mere minute of his advice.

So, maybe you feel let down and bubble-burst? "Oh man... If even the best astrologer can only be right 20% of the time... what's the use?"

Well, 20% accuracy is 10-20 times better advice about the future than you could usually get by intelligence alone! Consider this: How often is the weather forecast accurate - even with all their supercomputers? Not all that often. Maybe about 25% of the time? I mean they sort of get it basically right, but not the details, and not too far in the future, and sometimes they're just totally wrong. But we still listen to the weather reports, and they are still helpful! I personally think that the best astrologers can get similar accuracy as the weathermen. And I think that's pretty damn *amazing* when we consider that the mega-funding and supercomputing of modern meteorology is completely absent from modern astrology.

Don't be a gullible guppy gobbling pseudo-spiritual bravado from slippery sooth-sayers claiming 100% crystal-ball-priority-access to everything you might ever want to know in the past, present, or future. But also don't disregard the amazing potential to gain a far clearer comprehension of your life via consultation with an authentic, honest astrologer.

Chapter Three:
Change your Past

Time has no qualities of its own, so we can't perceive it directly, we can only perceive it indirectly through its effect: change. We infer the passage of time by perceiving changes, because that's what time *is*. Time is the enabler of change.

Change of position is a very basic type of change. We call it "motion." Motion and time, therefore, are inexorably related. Scientists like Einstein have noted this thoroughly.

When things don't change much, time seems to pass very slowly. When lots of things are changing, time flies. But time is not *entirely* subjective; it is also objective. No matter how bored or thrilled we are, there are still no more or less than twenty-four hours in a day. It may seem like each hour lasts for a year or a minute, but nonetheless the clock ticks off the same duration of twenty-four hours.

Why? How can time be both subjective and objective?

Our relative experience of time exists in our individual consciousness, as a result of our individual experience of change. Our individual consciousness, however, is a ray from the singular super-consciousness, *paramātmā,* a universal entity aware of all changes in all fields. Super-consciousness establishes synchronicity amongst relativity.

The "body" of the super-soul *paramātmā* is the universe itself. Motions in that body help express time in an objective way. The apparent motion of the Sun relative to the equator, for example, establishes the objective durations of days and years.

Three Phases of Time

We think of time as having three "phases" - past, present, and future, but this is not exactly true. The past and future don't actually exist, only the present does. The past is merely the present that was; the future merely the present that will be.

When something changes, we lose access to its previous state and it becomes "the past." The past is real only in so far as it continues to influence the present. For example when we hold ice, it melts. Its solid state disappears and becomes the past. Yet that past remains real because it influences the present – our hands are now cold.

When a change is potential, it is "the future." Like the past we have no access to it. Still, it is "real" to the extent that it affects our present. For example, if we want ice we can create that future by pouring water into an ice tray and putting it into a freezer.

So, the past and future are extensions of the present, and the present exists with its extensions within conscious perception. There are infinite individual conscious entities, so there are infinite pasts and futures. But, the super-consciousness *param-ātmā* establishes an objective past and future to which all the subjective pasts and futures synchronize and reconcile.

Now

The only moment that is truly real is the present. The realness of the past is only its echo of consequence. The realness of the future is only its seed of inspiration.

If we want to achieve enduring happiness and peace of mind we need to comprehend this as deeply as possible. Otherwise we will waste a huge portion of our life-energy lamenting over the past or worrying about the future.

Most often, we lament about the past because something went wrong and we can't change it. "My father scarred me for life." But if we realize that the past has no reality outside of its effect on the present, we will start to understand how we *can* change it.

Even if the past was great, we tend to lament anyway. "That was great, but now it's gone. Those were the good old days. Boo hoo." Yet, if we realize that the past remains real so long as it affects the present, we will experience that the past is never gone.

When we're not lamenting the past, we worry about the future. Is it worth it? The future isn't even real outside the inspiration it provides in the present. So, instead of worrying about the future, seize it. Change the way you utilize that inspiration, right here and now, and you gain the power to change your future.

We have the ability to change the past and future, by changing the way those two phases of time intersect with the only real moment: the present. . We can effectively change the past by changing how it affects our present. By taking charge of our present, we gain the power to *truly* re-write our past and re-design our future.

Three Phases, Three Modes

India's Veda informs us that the world has three fundamental properties that are the fundamental materials of all evolutions. Many people call these "The Three Modes." These Three Modes produce the perception that time has three phases.

The first mode is *sattva*. The word *sattva* means "realness." This mode grants clear access to reality, and engenders a natural sense of satisfaction and happiness. *Sattva* connects us to the present - the only real phase of time. Focusing on the present puts us in touch with *sattva* and thus tends to calm us down and clarify our thoughts.

The second mode is *rajas* - "colored." The light of consciousness does not shine as clearly though it, because the dust of passion and ambition color and tint it. *Rajas* makes consciousness perceive time as the future - the fantastic phase in which our ambitions might take shape and our dreams might come true. When we focus on the future we experience the effects of *rajas*: agitation and a passion/anxiety to achieve some new milestone or accomplish some new goal.

The third mode is *tamas* - "darkened." The light of consciousness doesn't shine much *at all* through this mode. Dark *tamas* facilitates forgetfulness and sleep. It causes consciousness to perceive time as the past, and makes us feel lethargic in the present, lazy about the future and prone to regret and anger.

Healthy Connection to Past and Future

Hearing that "only the present is real" we might overcompensate by embracing a philosophy that cares nothing for the past or future. This would be a mistake, for it would only narrow the consciousness. Enlightened consciousness comprehends all three phases of time; it does not ignore the past and future.

If we lose ourselves in the past, we will experience lethargic sadness and regret. But if we perceive the past with a present-centered focus, it will become a source of steady and patient wisdom born from experience.

If we lose ourselves to the future, we experience anxiety and emotional hunger. But if we perceive the future with present-focus, it will become a source of inspiration.

When we use astrology we should make a conscious effort not to get completely sucked into *rajas* and *tamas* by focusing excessively on the future or the past. Doing so invariably leads to "bad astrological trips," since *rajas* and *tamas* have no beneficial outcomes on their own. Thus many people leave a reading in anxiety (too much emphasis on the future), or depression (too much emphasis on the past). We must use astrology as a tool for improving our understanding of the present. Let the past and future inform and inspire the present. Stay present-focused.

Chapter Four:

The Original Religion?

We've explained a bit about how astrology, the science of telling time, is our "original science," but sometimes we also hear astrology called the "original religion." What does *that* mean? And how could astrology be both the original science and the original religion – aren't the two somewhat at odds with each other?

These days we misconstrue science and religion to be contrary beasts, but they're not. Religion and science are two approaches to the same issue: reality. Science strives to comprehend reality through observations and extrapolations. Religion strives for it by devotion and fealty. Astrology is at the ancient root of both. It is the root of science because it is the mother of observation and inference. And it is the root of religion because it is our original effort to place ourselves into better harmony with the reality of divine nature.

What is Religion?

For a long time now, religion has been a very misunderstood subject. Neither the religious nor the non-religious seem to have very many in their ranks who clearly understand what it really is. Let's see if we can make a dent in that.

Religion has two sides: ideal and practical. On the one side it is something transcendental, on the other, something mundane. The ideal, transcendental purpose of religion is comprehension of and harmonious unity with the divine root of reality. The practical, mundane purpose of religion, however, is simply government. Nothing regulates the masses as effectively as fear, and no fear is as effective as fear of all-powerful punishment by an absolute authority.

Religion, at its most practical, is simply conformity to a set of principles your community has decided to enforce. In most religions, these principles were decided in the distant past by very wise or special people (or are made to seem so) and are generally expressed as if they were the words of God, the absolute authority and all-mighty enforcer, or his unquestionable prophet and representative. This aspect of religion has the potential to be oppressive, but is not *inherently* evil. Government, organization, and regulation can (and very often do) enable us all to cooperate and co-exist.

Even with its totalitarian-inclined warts, government is only the mundane side of religion. Religion has another side, ideal and transcendent, focused on comprehending harmony and unity with the divine. Here, religion is not a tool to regulate society; it is a tool for individuals who seek the true nature of themselves, the world, and the source of both.

These days we are very tired of religion, because for a very long time religions have painfully and blatantly exploited their mundane purpose of controlling the masses, all the while becoming more and more destitute and inept in maintaining their functionality as viable paths to tangible God-realization. We don't even like to associate the word "religion" with it's higher function anymore. Instead we call the higher function of religion "spirituality." I sympathize and see the value in this distinction, but when we are considering why astrology is the original religion, let's keep

34

the original concept of the word, including both the mundane and ideal sides of the thing.

Astrology as Religion

The link between astrology and religion would not be clear if we think only of astrology in its modern fortune-telling form. But if we remember the original form of astrology - a science of knowing time – it becomes clearer.

Clocks and calendars are the original regulators of the masses, and the original means of communion with the divine. They are the original priests and priestesses of the original religion.

How do clocks and calendars put us in communion with the divine? By synchronizing with time, we synchronize with nature – for it is the movements of nature that define the objective passing of time. By synchronizing with nature, we synchronize with the divine, for nature is the most immediate and tangible form of divinity.

This may not always be evident in Western religious frameworks, beset as they are with a stark dualism between divine and mundane, body and soul, "this world" and "that world." But the divorce of nature from divinity is carefully avoided by almost all forms of Eastern religion. The sacred writings of the East consistently present the natural world as the first aspect of divinity with which we can interact and attain sacred union.

This non-dual worldview is expounded in the Bhāgavata Purāṇa – which is widely embraced as the ultimate evolution of eastern philosophical culture; being a thorough elaboration and explanation of Vedānta Sūtra, which is itself an extract of the essential knowledge in all the Upaniṣadas, which are themselves a clarification of the philosophical and spiritual import of the original Veda. The second division of this Purāṇa explores the realization of divinity *within* nature, explicitly identifying this as the first step towards full God-realization. Here is one relevant quote from the First Chapter of this section in the Bhāgavata, which I have translated from Sanskrit and published as a book titled "Creating the Creator."

> "Space is his navel. The directions are his ears and sound is his sense of hearing. Fragrance is his sense of smell. Blazing fire is his mouth; water, his palate; and flavor, his tongue. Dawn is his eyelid, the sun his eye, and brilliance is his vision. The movements of the Sun are his eyebrows. Oceans are his abdomen. Mountains are his bones. Rivers are his veins. Flora are the hairs on his body. The air is his infinitely powerful breath. Time is his movement. Rainclouds are the hair on his head. Twilight is his clothing. Matter itself is simply his power of cognition. All beings are simply his inner will."

Time itself, the main focus of astrology, is a very special part of the divine world. You will be hard pressed to find a more obviously omnipresent and omnipotent natural force. That is why time is, for most of us, the most immediate and tangible form of God. In Bhagavad Gītā, Krishna says, kālo'smi: "I am time." He identifies time as a divine representation of himself because everyone can directly perceive that time is the ultimate all-powerful controller.

Of course, the divine is much more than just this natural world, but that does not contradict the principle that the natural world is divine. A five-dollar bill is hardly all the money in the world, but it is still money. Time is not all that God is, but God is all that time is.

There's much, much, much more to the Supreme Reality than simply being an ultimate, all-powerful controller. The Upanishads declare, raso vai saḥ - "he is utmost ecstatic joy." This describes the transcendent nature of divinity, and those who have risen beyond selfish existence can experience it. But for all the rest of us mired in this dog-eat-dog realm, transcendent divine joy is not much within our grasp. For us, divinity is more obviously present in an imposing form - as

36

the supreme inconvenience, the inescapable limitation, the ultimate imposition: time.

Time is cold, hard, and rough. It looks ugly, at least on the outside. After saying "I am time," Krishna explains what time does, "It ends every beginning and destroys every creation." That paints a pretty bleak and awful picture, doesn't it? Why should the divine be so rough and destructive?

Loving parents also get stern sometimes. It looks rough and intrusive at first, to us kids. But when we grow up we understand it was love and protection. Time destroys our world, but our world is an illusion keeping us distracted from an infinitely more beautiful and fascinating reality.

Time destroys our illusions by imposing limits and endings, which on the scale of a lifetime take the form of old age, illness and death. These things have an undeniably awful smell and nightmarish glare. Our repulsion and fear of these things are not merely cultural impositions or Freudian snags. Even infants, animals, birds, and insects are instinctively gripped by this fear, as is every individual throughout every culture in every era of history. They are universally terrifying and disturbing because they threaten our *core* illusion, our most cherished fantasy: our ego.

Beneath our pretty skin and hair we are a mass of emotions and opinions spreading a blueprint of thoughts and schemes. Beneath even that we are "ego" - a concept of identity. Ego is the *core* of what we are, the eternally concomitant side-effect of consciousness. It is therefore extremely precious to every living being. Death, disease and old age are as frightening as they are not really because of what they do to the body, but because of what they do to the ego – they destroy the fundamental lies upon which our ego is built.

The fundaments of our ego rest in the great-granddaddy blueprint of all twisted ideas: that we are self-sufficient, competent, and capable; fit to be the central actor on the stage of life. Time comes along and plays a dissonant chord, threatening to completely destroy the dreamy tune our ego is busy whistling. Time makes it impossible to really believe that we are self-sufficient. In a few days we die without water. In a few weeks we die with food. In a few minutes we die without air. Time demonstrates that we are entirely dependent on nature. We cannot stop time from deteriorating, breaking and disintegrating our property. We cannot stop time from scattering and terminating the lives of our friends and relatives. We cannot even stop our own bodies from wearing out, becoming "old," and succumbing to death. Time erodes the foundations of our illusory ego, and is therefore the most frightening form our best friend could ever take.

Living things have an instinctual dislike of time and fear of death, but astrology encourages us to evolve beyond instinct and adopt a different attitude. It inspires us to work with time rather than struggle against it. "Become harmonious with time," she teaches. "Become harmonious with the power enforcing time. Let go of the ego that resists time's power. Embrace humility. Accept your supporting-role on the divine stage. Then you will feel much happier, know peace, and experience the passing of time with far more grace, even coming to see the positivity within it. Then you may even discover how to enter the infinite eternality within time."

Part 2
Fate & Freewill

Chapter Five:

Destiny is Beautiful.
Fate is Friendly.

Century after century we laid there gazing upward, observing the sky, learning how to stay in sync with nature by tracking the movements of the sun, moon, and planets. Day after day the sun followed the same pattern of rising and setting. Month after month the moon waxed and waned with the same rhythm. Year after year the sun crept northward and southward at the same pace, making the nights shorter and longer with constant tempo.

We saw *patterns* - steady, reliable, predictable patterns.

And this led us to conceive an amazing, inspiring idea: that the universe wasn't a jumble of chance whimsy and chaos. There was reason out there. There was sense. Things didn't just *happen* at random. Things happened according to plan, and things moved towards predictable destinations.

We thus discovered the concept of "destiny."

Destiny is a term for the concept that things in the world have specific, intended *destin*ations. Things do not happen by the whimsy of a quark or a god. They happen purposefully and abide by rational laws of cause and effect – as evidenced

41

fundamentally by the fact the universe moves in purposeful patterns.

Fate & Freewill

People have mixed feelings about destiny because they think it is at odds with the sacred notion of freewill. But freewill and fate are not at odds. They are not opposites. In fact *freewill creates fate.* Freewill doesn't contradict destiny. Freewill *creates* destiny.

I'll explain:

Let's say you and I don't know one another but are on the same bus, sitting next to each other, on a long ride somewhere. While I sit next to you I have the choice to either be rude or friendly. How I make this choice will affect the future. If I choose to act like a jerk, I create the destiny of being hated by you. If I choose to be helpful and friendly, I create the destiny of becoming your friend.

This is a simple illustration of how freewill creates fate; it creates the destination to which the future flows.

It's a simplified example. In truth you also have freewill, and can choose how to react to my freewill. And in truth both of our wills are conditioned and influenced by many factors. Nonetheless, the bottom line is freewill.

Destiny: An Expression of Divine Love

Choices lead to actions. Actions generate reactions. Sir Isaac Newton observed the symmetry of action and reaction as a physical principle, but the physics of it is just the tip of the iceberg. The entire universe, in every way, runs on the principle that actions generate reactions, choices generate repercussions. In Sanskrit the principle is known as *karma.*

Why does the universe operate by this principle? Why do choices generate reactions?

Well, because it's fair. I *should* be held accountable for my actions.

Why?

Because if I'm not held accountable, I will never change!

Well, so what?

Well, if I never change, I will never evolve.

Why should you want to evolve?

Because I am not as happy as I should be. I want to become happier than I am right now.

So, it all comes down to freewill seeking happiness. That is the true core of what existence itself is all about. The universe helps us find deeper and deeper happiness, by enforcing repercussions to our choices. Through these repercussions she dissuades us from behavior that doesn't truly lead to happiness and encourages us towards behavior that does. These repercussions are collectively known as destiny, and are actually an expression of universal, divine love.

Arguments Against

Some say, "There is no such thing as fate - everything is just random chance based on chaos."

The non-random patterns of the moon, sun and so on do not evidence chaos. What appears to be chaos is simply causality that exceeds the boundaries of our comprehension.

Some say, "Destiny is random, it has nothing to do with freewill or free choice."

Destiny *means* purposeful cause and effect. If destiny is random it's not *destiny*, it's *chance*. To say, "destiny is random" is to contradict oneself.

On the opposite end of the spectrum, some say, "Fate is absolute. Freewill is an illusion."

If so, we are all nothing more than robots hopelessly stuck in an eternal loop of causes and effects. If this is the case, destiny is a random and unjust (why should one robot get a different fate than another, if it has done nothing on its own to warrant anything of the sort?). And, as mentioned before, if destiny is random it's not destiny at all.

If I have no freewill I am merely a puppet of the forces that control me. Why then should I enjoy or suffer the repercussions of deeds done by my puppet master? It is meaningless to punish or reward someone for deeds someone else performs.

If a killer wears a glove while he stabs a victim, do we punish the glove? Do we punish the knife? These instruments were used in the murder, but they had no choice. Therefore there is no sense in punishing them.

If I am forced at gunpoint to take money from a cash register, with absolutely no choice in the matter at all, who will be put in jail – me, or the person who forced me at gunpoint? Justice does not hold anyone accountable for actions they did cause. If I am punished at all, it will be because justice will not believe that I could possibly have absolutely no choice in the matter.

If, "the butler killed the mistress in the drawing room with a candlestick," who is responsible for the murder - the butler, the drawing room, or the candlestick? The butler go to jail while the candlestick and drawing room get off Scott-free.

Why? Because the butler is a person, the candlestick and drawing room are not. What's the difference between a person and a candlestick? One has sentient *will*, and the other doesn't. Will causes action, and action generates repercussions for the cause of the action. In short, the butler is responsible for the murder, because the murder happened as a result of his willful choice.

Logic insists that the cause is responsible for the effect. The effect is destiny. If it's *my* destiny, the cause must be *me* – not a cosmic dice roll.

Some will say, "To hell with logic. The universe is meaningless and irrational."

Well, sorry, but that's nonsense. We've watched the skies for centuries and we know that the universe *is* rational because it shows us reasonable, methodical patterns.

"Freewill causes fate." This is the only conclusion that remains faithful to the original observations of order in the universe, observations which inspired the concept of destiny and fate in the first place.

The Sanskrit word most often used for "destiny" is *karma*. But karma is more than an Eastern synonym for fate. Karma is a single word that simultaneously denotes action *and* reaction, thus beautifully expressing the inseparability of action and reaction, the unity between cause and effect, and the symbiosis between freewill and fate.

The Universe: Our Mother, or a Slot Machine?

We make choices, and are held accountable for them. This is the only rational conclusion faithful to the original observations of order in the universe, observations which generated the concept of destiny in the first place, but *who* or *what* holds us accountable for our choices?

45

The universe. The divine universe herself observes all our free choices as a firsthand witness and holds us accountable to their rewards and punishments.

OK... but why?

Because she cares about us.

Why does she care about us?

Because we are her children!

How does her enforcing our destiny show that she cares about us?

It shows that she is our mother trying to help us grow up.

We human beings are not infants among the life forms. We are adolescents, at least. Children get away with all sorts of outlandish things: breaking dishes, spilling stuff, drawing on walls, you name it - because they don't really know any better. They don't really have much choice yet. But a young adult begins to know better. He is given greater freedom, and greater choice - which means greater responsibility, and greater accountability.

The universe is the mother of all life forms. When she produces a human being she wants to see the soul therein avail herself of the rare opportunity to evolve more fully into spiritual adulthood. Karma is her parenting technique.

What kind of "evolution" am I talking about? I mean the only kind that really matters, the evolution towards happiness. Evolving and "growing up" (spiritually) means to get a clearer idea of what happiness is, and how to live within it. The universe provides us a realm in which we can search for happiness. She guides our search through karma: rewarding our choices when they are more conducive to true happiness, and punishing the choices that interfere with attaining that goal. Karma is an ingenious way to gradually bring us to higher levels of happiness, at our own pace, without violating our freewill.

We can describe "growing up" as the process of "learning lessons." So, what lesson does our Universal Mother teach us through fate? It is the one lesson pointed towards by all the other lessons ever learned by anyone at any places or time in history. It is the ultimate lesson. It is this:

Happiness does not exist outside you.

Happiness exists within you.

But what is "inside us"? Inside us is an infinite emotional energy, which like all forms of energy, needs to flow to a proper terminus. It is, ultimately, love. When we say, "Happiness exists within us," we mean that happiness exists in the natural loving propensity of the soul.

What is Love?

The great sage of transcendental love, Rūpa Goswāmī, brilliantly and succinctly defined love as, "Expression of the desire to please someone." He said that when there is no ulterior motive in expressing this desire, it is *pure* or *true* love. And he said that when the energy of love flows to the supreme, All-Attractive target ("Krishna") it is *transcendental* true love.

Love is the opposite of selfishness. We can't really experience love while the thorny blanket of selfishness envelopes us; and so long as we can't experience love, we can't really experience happiness; and so long as we can't really experience happiness, we miss the whole point of existence.

That's why nothing is as important to our happiness as getting rid of the selfish ego. And that's what time and destiny is all about. That's *why* the universe exists and functions by the law of karma: to help us get free from the

47

selfish world-view we choose to adopt, a world-view that cripples us from truly existing in a state of actual happiness. By rewarding our less selfish choices with pleasant repercussions, and punishing our more selfish choices with distressing repercussions, karma guides us towards true happiness. So, our distress is not meaningless. We do not suffer randomly, or without purpose. The purpose of distress is to dissuade us from continuing to do selfish things - because selfishness is antithetical to true happiness.

I'm Not Selfish!

"What!? I'm not selfish! Certainly not selfish enough to warrant the types of distress I've been put through!"

Though some of us suffer far more extreme distress than others, we all feel this way at least at one point or another in our lives. It is a reflexive self-defense mechanism of the selfish ego. It's our inner armor against humiliation.

For most all of us, it's pretty humiliating to think that we deserve the life we often lead. That's why there is a psychological gatekeeper in the mind who locks away nearly all our memories and puts a soft "me-favorable" focus on our perception of the present. Our mind stores limitless memories from this life and previous lifetimes, but the gatekeeper blocks access to memories that contradict our ego's cherished image of itself, memories that would disable our self-absolving notion that we don't deserve any bad things. The gatekeeper even works on present perceptions as a monumental information filter rapidly reinterpreting reality in such a way that we are never really the one to blame for anything.

The gatekeeper is our ego's best friend, and the main reason why it can take eons and eons to "grow up."

It would be terrifying to remove the information filter on our past and present, and see in Technicolor just how awful and

48

selfish we really are. Even the most trivial daily affairs would suddenly reveal their bloodstains. For example, most of us cause an enormous amount of needless pain and death just by eating lunch! If we open our minds and hearts with the key of humility we suddenly become aware of many, many extremely selfish things we do. Suddenly it doesn't seem so preposterous that what happens to us is meant to happen to us, even the serious difficulties in our life.

There are no malfunctions in the gears of destiny. It is exact and perfect, and even our distress is a beneficial, intentional experience, a necessary catalyst of evolution out of a selfish state of being that robs us of the true bliss of existence. The pleasant things in our lives are also meaningful, not just for "fun," but because they can help us more regularly gravitate towards less selfish deeds.

Thus, *fate is friendly*, in both its smiling and scowling mask.

Reincarnation?

I alluded to previous lifetimes. Reincarnation is an essential topic in the discussion of astrology and destiny. Perhaps there are still many people in the West who view reincarnation as an outlandish, irrational concept. However, just as karma has a dimension that can be empirically measured in the physical world, reincarnation has a similar tangible dimension: the law of Conservation of Energy. This physical law states that, "Energy is never created or destroyed, it merely changes state."

Life is a type of energy: consciousness. This life-energy, like all other forms of energy, is never created or destroyed - it eternally exists. Birth is not it's beginning and death is not it's end. Birth and death are just significant "changes of state" for life-energy, which constantly changes state. Sometimes we experience these changes on a small scale as growth, sometimes on a bigger scale as evolution, and sometimes on the largest personal scale as birth and death.

Life-energy changes state because it carries karma. Destiny records that we need to experience certain conditions, and thus requires us to change our state, and transform into situations capable of experiencing those conditions. Without karma, life-energy can exit in a perpetual state, without change. Attaining this permanent state is the initial goal of spiritual evolution, called *mokṣa*. Karma itself works to ferry us gradually towards that goal.

Since the ancient, beginningless past, we have made countless decisions and performed countless acts, and therefore carry the momentum of countless karmas. That is why we are born with specific destinies.

As soon as we are born and take our first breath, our hearts and minds begin melding into their new nervous system, integrating into their new body. With each breath we identify more solidly with the new body, and forget more thoroughly all traces of our previous lives. This happens out of necessity. If we were consciously aware of having previously identified with so many other bodies and identities, how deeply could we invest our consciousness yet again into a new situation - certainly doomed to the same limitations and eventual changes of state? So, for the sake of fitting the heart and mind into the current body, the memories of previous bodies are locked away by the mind's gatekeeper.

People who make efforts not to identify too deeply with their current body develop greater access to memories of previous lifetimes.

You could argue that since the common person can't recall the deeds of their previous life, it's pointless and ineffective to reward or punish them for those deeds. Punishment and reward, you could argue, is not very effective when the subject is not aware of the connection between the cause and effect.

It's true that karma would be much more effective if we were more aware of the connections between our deeds and their reactions. But it's not true that reward and punishment is

50

completely ineffective if the subject is not directly conscious of the cause of their reward or punishment. Although the progress is much slower, karma still acts as an evolutionary catalyst on our subconscious, even when the conscious mind employs selective perception to block and alter the past and present.

In fact, hiding the cause from those who want it hidden is a A special genius of the karmic mechanism – which never violates freewill. But the thoughtful who seek true, objective knowledge can figure out the causes by the effects. A person dying at the hands of a murderer, for example, need not be consciously aware of the countless times they killed other living beings in this lifetime and in previous lifetimes. If they are willing, within the experience itself they can see the negative nature of murder - and thus receive the opportunity to accept a very powerful impetus for reform and evolution.

Chapter Six:

The Architect of Destiny

Since time out of mind, people have been beset with the misconception that something other than freewill is at the root of fate. This misconception does not spare even the majority of people who love astrology. Indeed even a great deal of serious astrologers are themselves under its sway, promoting the irrational idea that stars and planets have some sort of "influence," "power" or "control" over us.

Our moods don't change because of body-water being tugged by the moon. If body-water is that *sensitive* to variations, then drinking a Perrier or standing on your head should hit us like a full smack of LSD. The sun's "rays" don't influence our career. If they did, the equator and the beach would be the financial and industrial hot-spots of the world! Sun-rays will give you sunburn 40 zillion times faster than they will give you a promotion. Protons, neutrons, gravitons, time-waves, space-waves, pulsars, quasars, zig-zag zeldars and every other sort of marklar-ray from globs of rocks and gas billions of parsecs away do not create your personality type, affect your life, or decide whether or not your will win the lottery.

If it all comes down to freewill, what's astrology all about? Is it a sham?

No. In real astrology the planets and stars are *symbols* that *indicate* our nature and destiny, not forces that control us and determine who and what we are.

The divine universe enforces fate, and the stars and planets are parts of that universe. They are important parts because they are the parts we can see; much like the hands on a clock are the observable protrusions of the much more complex clockwork beneath. The hands of a clock don't cause the clock to run, but they allow people to read the clock. Similarly, the planets (hands of the universal clock) move through the zones of space (the face of the universal clock). Karma is the clockwork that runs the universe, but the positions of planets and stars in the sky offer humanity a way to read the karmic forecast.

The configuration of planets at the time of your birth, for example, reveals something about how the universe is configured towards you, and thus provides a symbol you can decode to understand what karmic fruits the universe will bestow to you during this lifetime.

Why should the universe put "hands" on its "clock-face"?

Out of love.

The universe exists because of divine love for us. She is our mother. A mother communicates with her children, out of love. There are limitless ways for the divine universe to communicate with us; astrology is one. If the universe is the body of our divine mother, astrology is like her "body language" (or shall we say "*sign* language"). By observing the sky, we hear our mother's confirmation that there *is* rhyme and reason out there, there *is* a purpose to the events in the world and in our lives. Someone universal is taking care of us, ushering us towards deeper happiness, although our reluctance to cooperate makes it sometimes feel very difficult and stressful.

Mascara on Ugly Eyes

I admit, there is a strong appeal in denying the centrality of freewill. If neutrinos and fickle gods sprinkling space dust forced me to be the person I am, then they are to blame the mess I'm so often in – and that sounds very nice to my ego.

Our current astrological culture is so seeped in this kind of mumbo-jumbo because we are 5,000 years into an age of decline. The ancient sciences and mystical technologies practically came to complete extinction by the time the Renaissance stepped in as the new hero. That hero, however, was more interested in inventing new sciences than rediscovering ancient ones.

The Renaissance rise of modern science combined with the ruination of ancient knowledge made it really hard, if not impossible, to logically defend the plausibility of astrology, and thus astrology rapidly lost credibility. Initially it was as respected a science as geometry, chemistry, mathematics and so on, but in the centuries immediately following the Renaissance, most people wrote astrology off as yet another hallucination of the dark years of yore.

Few of those who remained involved with astrology hailed from a logical, systematic, or truly scientific background. These remnant tried their best to validate astrology to the modernizing post-renaissance world, but most of what they came up with was plagiarism of science-vocabulary without science-logic. This situation persists today, and we find the internet overcrowded with astro-babble that plasters science-jargon onto irrational theories like makeup plastered on an ugly girl. Reestablishing the respectability of astrology is not something that will soon be endorsed by Harvard and the like. It is something that must begin at the grassroots level. If individuals like you and I can grasp the beautifully rational philosophy and science of astrology, hope remains that, one day, the science may return to the world in true form.

We must start by establishing the rational basis of destiny: cause is responsible for effect. *I* create *my* destiny. Planets explain and foretell it, but they do not create or control it – neither by their old-fashioned blessings and curses, nor by their modernized gravitons and neutrinos.

Until we embrace the fact that we are composed of will, we cannot embrace the truth that we are divine. To be *divine* means to have consciousness, and consciousness expresses itself as will. To really embrace our divinity we must accept responsibility for the situations we find ourselves in, and stop shoveling the blame onto other things and other people. We are *not* under the control of stars, planets, gods, aliens, lizard-men, lizards, political leaders, bosses, or our next-door neighbor's dog.

Instrumental Causes

"I am responsible for my destiny." This outlook is uplifting yet depressing; humbling yet empowering. It's humbling and depressing because it means I have no one to blame except myself. But it's also very uplifting and empowering because it informs me that I have all the power I'll ever need to eventually create the destiny I truly desire: uninterrupted loving happiness.

What about all the people who oppressed and exploited, assaulted and violated, and belittled and humiliated us, don't they have some power over us?

They *do* play a role and acquire guilt. But their role is instrumental, not causal. They are *instrumental* causes of our pain and suffering.

What's "instrumental"? A guitar is an instrument. Think about what a guitar does, and you'll understand what an "instrumental cause" is. Did a guitar cause the music Jimi Hendrix created? No, the artist is the cause. The guitar is an instrument the artist used.

56

All the vile people we have to deal with in this world are instruments, not causes, of pain and suffering.

Practical Alchemy

It's true that we are the architects of our own destiny, but it gets sticky in the timing. After all, we can't literally change something we've already done.

Lets say I slapped you yesterday. Today I feel awful about it, but can I change what I did? No. It's not that I don't have freewill, it's that I already used my freewill to slap you, and what's done is done. It has become the past and slipped beyond my access.

Yet, the past is only real in terms of how it affects the present. So there *is* a way I can change it. I can't change the fact that I slapped him, but I *can* change the way that past affects the present: I can apologize, for example. We can't wrestle the past into a different shape than what it was, but we can take charge of the present to build a better future.

"Good" and "Bad"

If I win ten million dollars, is that "good"? Usually, but it might not be if that money turns me into a snobby elitist and completely screws up my relationships with my children, friends, and so on. If I become poor, is that bad? Usually, but maybe not if it inspires me to discover the treasures freely available everywhere in life.

"Good" and "bad," "better" and "worse" – these are relativities. The goodness of a thing is relative to how beneficial it is to a particular goal. If I want to build a table, for example, a hammer is good. If I want to fix a computer, a hammer is bad. A big mistake we make almost all the time is to get caught up in worrying about our external resources:

whether we are going to get a hammer or blow dryer or a bottle of orange juice. We bite our nails and study the stars to see if our resources might become "good" sometime soon. The truth is that *any* resource is good, if we know how to use it! If I get a hammer, I'll build a tree house. If I get a blow dyer, I'll wash my hair and dry it. If I get a bottle of orange juice, I'll take a break and enjoy a refreshing drink. The only way anything can be bad is if I can't or won't find a good objective for it. If I insist on still wanting to drink when the universe is putting hammers in my hand, it's going to be bad.

Life can be really difficult sometimes. I'm not unaware of that, unfortunately. But even in the most challenging situations, the best remedy is to search for proper objective. We can't change what destiny gives us today, but we can always change our goals to match our resources. If we do, we will *always* be prosperous.

Prosperity doesn't arise from having specific resources, it arises from the ability to match resources to objectives. We simply need to be willing to switch objectives from building to hairdressing to snacking depending on what resources destiny provides to us. But there's a much deeper level to this. If we really want to be consistently and profoundly happy, we need to make our goal the same as the goal of our divine mother, the universe. We must decide to approach life as an opportunity to evolve under her expert guidance, and we must use *any* resource we get to further ourselves towards that goal.

A good astrologer helps us embrace destiny and align our goals with the potentials available in our resources. Amazing predictions are a pretty bunch of bells and whistles, but they don't make anyone any happier at the end of the day. Aligning your goals with the universe might not be as exciting as a Nostradamean decree, but it liberates us from all distress, and that's worth more than all the bells and whistles in the world.

Astrology is not here to help us avoid bad things, because, ultimately, there is no such thing as a bad thing.

58

Chapter Seven:

Crime & Punishment

A criminal likes to think of the police as the enemy who landed him in the slammer, but the truth is that his freewill got him locked up.[1] Criminal decisions lead to criminal actions, and criminal actions lead to criminal punishment. The laws and the enforcers of the laws are merely instrumental. The freewill behind the decision is the true cause.

Sure, if a criminal grew up in difficult circumstances it's understandably difficult for him *not to* use his freewill in criminal ways. Nonetheless, difficult to avoid or not, it's still freewill that agrees to hold a gun. In the end its *his* finger that pulls the trigger, moved by his muscles, commanded by his nervous system, controlled by his brain, operated by his consciousness – expressing his will. Although we often find ourselves almost forced to behave in certain ways, pushed relentlessly by the momentum of our psychological dispositions, still it is our responsibility to struggle against that momentum with our freewill.

---

[1] The police may abuse their power when the government is weak and corrupt, but the universe is all-powerful and does not permit corruption in her agents.

In the ultimate picture, even the "uncontrollable conditions" we are born into are the result of free choices we've made in countless previous lifetimes. So long as we feel too weak to fully embrace the power and centrality of our individual freewill, for that long we will continue to feel completely swept away by seemingly uncontrollable circumstances. But when we are ready to bravely take the wheel of our own lives, we can finally get somewhere.

Karma Kills Compassion?

It may seem cruel to say that criminals "deserve" to be incarcerated. If criminals deserve incarceration, and even deserve the difficult circumstances they were born into, then maybe the victims of crimes also deserve it? And why stop there? Maybe the people in extreme hunger and poverty deserve that, too?

It is cruel to think that way, I agree, even though, objectively speaking, it's not untrue. So I would like to offer a paradigm that maintains the veracity of universal justice without losing the virtue of compassion:

Karma gives us exactly what we deserve – yet we don't "deserve" to have karma in the first place.

In our natural state, we have the potential to be entirely free of karma. Thus, by our constitutional nature, we do not "deserve" to suffer. We deserve to experience the joy of existence. As a result of will, we're out of touch with our natural, constitutional state of being and therefore subject to karma, which in turn means we wind up deserving and even needing to suffer.

This understanding of karma doesn't kill compassion. In fact, it *expands* compassion to everyone. It's relatively common to feel compassion for the handicapped, the homeless, the hungry, and so on, but when we understand karma correctly we can feel compassion for *everyone*, all the time. Everyone in

60

this world is or has been selfish by exploiting other entities for their own gain. Everyone therefore has unpleasant karma to suffer. It's only a matter of time. The people who are destitute today are the people getting rid of their old karmic debts. The people who are irresponsibly opulent and powerful today are only getting rid of their *good* karma, creating or maintaining karmic debts that will soon come due. Ultimately, *everyone* suffers. So our compassion should expand to everyone.

A thorough understanding of karma also enables us to be humanitarian in substantially more real and effective ways. When I was a teenager I went into a convenience story in Berkley, California, after walking past a destitute person sitting by the door begging for change. I bought a loaf of bread and offered it to him.

"I need money," he quipped, "not bread."

I took back the bread and didn't give him any money. If food wasn't a priority in his condition, obviously he didn't need money for anything good. We can't just throw "compassion" at people and they will actually *benefit* from it. There are better ways to help a drug addict than throwing a 20 dollar bill into his tin can. When we understand karma in the right context, we will understand how to truly benefit everyone. In addition to whatever immediate practical emergencies need to be addressed, we have to help people see the personal ruination that comes from selfishness. Selfishness leads to the suffering of others, which generates suffering for oneself. To help others understand this is the ultimate form of philanthropy.

We should become, like the planets themselves, agents helping our Universal Mother raise her children, helping the people of the world gradually become less and less selfish, so they can eventually exit the realm of karma altogether and become situated in their constitutionally blissful condition as a selfless lover of the divine, All-Attractive Person. That is the ultimate altruism. If we engage in such charitable deeds, the universe sees no need to reform us through the standard

61

karmic mechanism - we are already reforming ourselves! That is the secret to deleting stockpiles of karma.

Victims & Criminals

We must not let the forked-tongued exploit the concept of karma to justify their own wrongs. "I am abusing you because you deserve it," they claim, overly or not. "I am not at fault, you are."

What nonsense!

Yes, the so-called victim experiences punishment as a result of all the abuse he or she has inflicted in the past, but no sane person would ever volunteer to be the agent dispensing that punishment! What can be gained from that, except the guarantee of one's future position on the receiving end of the same torment and abuse one dishes out? He who kills is killed; He who torments is tormented; He who exploits is exploited. Therefore what sane person would kill, torment, or exploit?

So, when someone tyrannizes us with the idea that we deserve their abuse, we can respond with a compassionate laugh, saying, "I guess you are right. I must deserve this. But do *you* deserve it too? Because by volunteering to be the instrument inflicting this suffering, you have qualified yourself to experience the very same abuse. For your sake, not mine, you should desist."

Evil people do not materialize out of thin air. Evil people come from evil situations. The victim of evil perpetrates evil, when he or she submits their will to the selfish reflex to retaliate. Thus the victim becomes the criminal. And what then becomes of the criminal? He soon becomes the victim. The criminal generates an environment of crime, in which he or she inevitably becomes a victim. If circumstances don't allow this to manifest immediately, the karma will follow the criminal even more tenaciously and viciously through lifetimes.

The victim/criminal cycle does not end unless we apply our freewill. We need to muster the willpower to stop our impulse to be evil to others just because others were evil to us.

Victims of evil can perhaps find some solace in the outlook that it is actually more unfortunate to be the criminal than the victim. When we are the victim at least we are releasing a negative karmic reaction. If we are the criminal we only create the same. Immediate punishment is better for the criminal. Unpunished crime causes suffering that endures far longer and bites far more intensely, because the karmic mechanism is indirect and therefore requires greater force to achieve the same result.

A Nasty World?

If the universe is a mother who loves her children, why is the world such a nasty place? Well, childhood ain't a bed of roses, you know. There's an awful lot of crying and screaming involved in growing up. Most of those tears come from not being able to tell the difference between "good" and "nice." Things can be good without being nice, and they can be nice without being good. Dieting, for example, isn't nice but it is a good way to advances towards our health-goals. Candy, on the other hand, is very nice... but not very good for health.

A mom insists, "No video games until your homework is finished!"

A child might react by thinking, "Mom is bad!"

Young children seldom have goals beyond the next five minutes. That's why rules, restrictions, and reprimands never feel nice to a child. A mother, however, is a mature adult (we hope). Her goals for the child aren't limited to five minutes of fun, they are focused on years and years of the child's of wellbeing. So she knows that her regulations are good for the child, even though the child complains and resists.

As a child grows up, he gradually starts to understand his mother's point of view. He starts to feel grateful for the effort mom put into raising him. He starts to regulate and govern himself - needing less correction and restriction from his mother. Parent and child both become so much happier.

For how many more billions of years will we remain spiritually childish?

To mature as children of the universe, the first step is to accept the concept that the universe is motherly and has our best interest in mind. We should try to realize that even the not-nice things in our lives are not meant to be bad. We only make them bad by resisting the important changes they try to inspire within us.

Chapter Eight:

The Beginning of Everything

"The universe is our loving mother." Sounds nice, but why should the universe love us? Answering this takes us back to the beginningless beginning of all beginnings.

एको बहु स्यात्

eko bahu syāt

**The One
shall be many.**

"The One" is an infinite singularity. Expressing the infinite plurality inherent in its singularity, the One becomes many.

United plurality is better than absolute singularity. Imagine yourself all alone, as the only entity in existence. It would certainly get pretty lonely and boring, wouldn't it? Even if you had all of everything latent within you, it would be dull unless all that diversity within you could become manifest and tangible.

The One becomes many because The One prefers bliss over boredom, just like we do.

The Upanishads repeatedly describe The One as आनन्दमय (*ānanda-maya*) "The entity of ecstasy." Ecstasy is not enjoyed alone! This is why the very nature of The One is to manifest as Many.

There is something like a spiritual "big bang" by which the infinite singularity of The One manifests infinite plurality as The Many. Countless souls – including you and me – spring into existence from it. It's not a destructive explosion; the One does not cease to exist when it fragments into The Many. The One exists even more definitely and gloriously after expanding into The Many, as The One around whom The Many revolve, like many stars revolving around the center of a galaxy or the many planets revolving around the sun.

This is why the Upanishads make statements like:

ॐ

पूर्णमदः पूर्णमिदं पूर्णात्पूर्णमुदच्यते ।
पूर्णस्य पूर्णमादाय पूर्णमेवावशिष्यते ॥

oṁ
pūrṇam adaḥ pūrṇam idaṁ pūrṇāt pūrṇam udacyate
pūrṇasya pūrṇam ādāya pūrṇam evāvaśiṣyate.

Oṁ
From that infinite whole comes this infinite whole.
Completeness generates completeness.
When completeness comes from completeness,
completeness remains.

No matter what you subtract from infinity, the result is still infinite. Even if you subtract infinity from infinity, infinity remains. So, The One remains intact and whole, and generates The Many as infinite intact wholes.

Why bother? Bliss.

The One becomes many for the sake of expanding infinite bliss. If we digest this carefully the meaning of life will no longer seem like an impossible conundrum for armchair philosophers, it will suddenly become clear and beautifully simple:

Why do we exist?

Because The One became many.

Why?

To amplify the bliss of existence.

Then, what is the meaning of life?

The meaning and purpose of life is to amplify the bliss exchanged between The One and The Many. The meaning of life is joy, and the ultimate form of joy is love, so, ultimately, the meaning of life is love, especially the love exchanged between The Many and The One.

Opting Out

When we amplify the loving bliss-circuit that emanates from and returns to The One, then we truly, fully exist. When we divorce ourselves from that function, we exist in a pseudo-reality of vain attempts to amplify our own self-centered bliss.

We don't *have to* function the way we were intended to function. We have intrinsic freewill, and are allowed to be uncooperative with the divine plan. We can "file for divorce," and a few of us do. Divorced from The One, we set out to be the center of our own universe.

Why does this happen?

It's not a mistake, its part of what makes love real. Love must be *willingly given,* and that is impossible unless we are allowed to be uncooperative. Without freewill, love is just a shallow word. And without real love, existence is pointless.

We who choose not to revolve around the bliss of The One are not "mistakes" to be "fixed." Our complexities can be resolved, but only by our own accord. That blossoming itself is part of the amplification of divine bliss, and therefore is part of the original plot, not something to be edited out!

The One gives us space and time (literally) to follow our independent inclinations. He thinks along these lines, "If The Disharmonious Few stay in this reality with their current wills, the symphony of ecstatic bliss enjoyed by The Many will be damaged by their dissonance. I will make another venue for their song. When they tire of the their independent soloing, I will help them turn towards the symphony of bliss, in the dance of The Many with The One.

"I will never violate their freewill, because without freewill, love is impossible; and without love, bliss is impossible; and without bliss existence is pointless. I will not change them, but I will give them the power to change themselves if they ever want to.

"The principles of existence will enforce themselves with absolute neutrality and impartiality. Thus, where multiple centers exist, there is sure to be conflict. Yet even this conflict is ultimately good, for it will reveal the need to locate the true center of existence, inspiring them to partake of their intended role in our infinite exchange of pure joy."

Part 3
Divination

Chapter Nine:

How to Use Astrology

As you start exploring the branches and leaves of destiny's details, it will be easy to forget where the forest lies on the cosmic map. If you forget the ultimate benefic purpose of fate itself, astrology will land you in the midst of a terrifying jungle where you regret the past, feel overwhelmed by the present, and are helpless about your future. If you remember the big picture, astrology will guide you closer to the harbor at the end of fate's river; the ultimate destination of the karmic flow: transcendent, selfless love. Remembering that *everything* in your destiny - "good" or "bad" - can propel you towards this destination, you need not ever lament the past, dread the present or fear the future.

Resist the doomed impulse to control the destiny you have already created. Instead, embrace the power you truly do have in the present and allow destiny to inspire you towards a more ideal future. Those who cling to astrology in hopes of sidestepping the knockout punches of destiny merely trip over their own two feet and knock themselves out. But the hearts of those who use astrology to more fully embrace the path destiny paves quickly find the harbor of divine bliss.

Never forget or nurture any doubt that the entire forest of fate grows from the soil of freewill. And while forests of terrible destiny will grow from the soil of self-centered will, blissful gardens will blossom from the soil of selflessly loving will.

Now, let's discuss how to get (and give) good astrological readings, consistently. Three things are essential: education, trust, and communication. Without *education* about what astrology is and isn't, our experience with it is going to be more "miss" than "hit." Without *trust* in our astrologer, we won't listen carefully and deeply enough to their words of wisdom. Without fluent *communication*, questions and answers will be misunderstood.

Education

The querent and the astrologer are, unfortunately, seldom on the same page, mainly because the astrologer knows tons and tons about astrology and the querent, in comparison, doesn't. So, a lot of energy is wasted in every reading because the astrologer has to reiterate the fundamental contexts (what destiny really is, what astrology really is, and what the fundamental symbols represent). Or even if the astrologer skips all the explanations and jumps straight to the interpretive conclusions – when the querent has no familiarity with the nature of the symbolism involved, the meaning and applicability of the information in the reading narrows and becomes crippled.

If you read this book a few times and discuss it with others, you will start to really comprehend the true nature of astrology, fate, and freewill. This will put you on the right page *with the right astrologers* (and fortuitously take you off the wrong page with the wrong astrologers). I will have similar books about all the essential symbols involved in astrology - the planets, signs and houses - and the essential mechanisms by which they interact with one another. It is very important for everyone, not just astrologers, to become at least a bit familiar with these things.

Trust & Trustworthiness

The most important part of asking a question is receptivity to the answer. The depth of our receptivity to an answer depends on the depth of our confidence in the person giving the answer. If we're absolutely convinced that the person we're inquiring from absolutely comprehends the topic of inquiry, we will naturally have absolute receptivity to the answers they give.

How much confidence do you have in your astrologer? You don't have to pretend that the astrologer is God, or a god, or even that he or she has the Skype IDs of the gods and angels, but you do at least have to be firmly convinced that the astrologer knows an awful lot more than you do, not only about astrology but also about karma, and about life in general.

It's also important that you know they're not uneducated about the specific topic you're inquiring about. If you have financial concerns, you need an astrologer who knows astrology *and* is knowledgeable in finance. If you have marriage concerns think twice about approaching an astrologer who can't maintain a solid marriage, even if that person might know a lot about astrology.

The astrologer acts in the role of your advisor, so you should take it pretty seriously and not just flit about from one astrologer to the next. Examine a wide sample of astrologers until you find someone who:

- Knows a lot more about the astrological science than the rest of the bunch.

- Knows a lot more about karma and philosophy than the rest of the bunch.

- Knows a good deal about the subjects that concern you.

- Doesn't lack some natural repartee with you, so that honest, straightforward communication isn't too difficult.

It's not going to be easy to find such a person, because you have to deserve it. You have to show your sincerity by educating yourself and searching thoroughly. Then the universe will provide a trustworthy guide.

Once you find a trustworthy guide, why mess around with others? Stick faithfully to one, and you will find that your comprehension of their unique use of words and symbols deepens and thus the effective communication of wisdom between the two of you becomes easier and more natural. If you go to many astrologers, you will just confuse yourself, even if they are all good astrologers, because everyone has their own way of seeing and expressing things. Take your time to find the right astrologer for you, and then stick with that astrologer and deepen your relationship as a recipient of his or her guidance and wisdom. The more you do this, the more fluid and effective the communication will become.

Never get a reading – not even a cheap or free one – from someone who is obviously uneducated or lacks wisdom. Don't listen to what such people say about you or about astrology. Don't subject yourself to most of the garbage written on most of the garbage websites and in most of the garbage newspaper and magazine columns out there. It will not only confuse you, it will weaken your trust in astrology as a whole.

Once you get a reading, how will you evaluate it?

That's a real kicker, isn't it – because, unless you are a learned astrologer and wise soul, it will not be easy to immediately evaluate the merits of a reading. Yet, you can take recourse to this essential principle: the most important, simple, and self-evident evaluation of the merit of a reading is how well it helps you transform yourself towards being a more selfless, loving, naturally happy person.

Once you find an astrologer whom you deeply respect and who gives you beneficial readings, you are in an extremely rare and fortunate position. Cherish it. Become fully receptive to the answers you receive from him or her. Meditate on your readings with faith that great truths are contained in them. Then, great truths will come to you from the Divine, often beyond what even the astrologer comprehended when giving you the reading.

Communication

Don't expect the astrologer to spell everything out in black and white for you the first time every time. Limitations on the efficiency of communication make that impossible, even if nothing else stands in the way. Listen to the astrologer communicate the essential astrological symbols and describe his or her vision of how they combine to affect your life. Then, make dialog to discover the clearest, most detailed import in what the astrologer sees.

Learn how to be interactive with the reading and with your astrologer!

Even if the interactive dialog is only an internal one within yourself, it is essential. After all, within yourself is the Divine, the source of all knowledge and wisdom. Our guides are merely instruments and conduits for the Divine.

Astrological symbols combine to present nearly infinite possibilities, all of which coexist in an order of prominence. If you don't understand the relevance or meaning of something your trusted astrologer explains, ask! He or she can almost always express the same symbolism in a slightly different permutation which more easily reveals its immediate relevance to you.

Chapter Ten:

How to Ask Questions

Don't try to make an astrologer say what you want to hear, asking the same question 100 different ways until you hear an answer that suits you.

Don't insist on more detail than what comes naturally. The level of detail you want is often not a level of detail you need, and might not even be a level of detail that even exists yet in the semi-solid future.

Sometimes good and explicit details will come leaping out of a horoscope, "Invest in Silver starting June 8th, 2017," "Go to a bookshop in your hometown and find the man wearing a purple shirt, you will marry him," etc. Sometimes this type of stuff comes to the astrologer, but when it *doesn't*, don't march into your horoscope with a wrench and suction cup trying to force it out. If the astrologer is experienced and expert, yet clear information still does not come out from a horoscope it means no clear information is *available* - the details you seek are not significant enough to be firmly determined, they could happen in many different ways.

It's not that astrology can't figure out specific details. It's that these details are often not important enough to be clearly and exactly specified in destiny's blueprint. It's not so much that astrology is "limited" in what it can perceive, but that reality is "unlimited" in how it can deliver the results of destiny. "What happened to me on March, 26, 1994?" or "What will happen to me on April 10, 2023?" If we ask questions like this we're not likely to get far, because most of the time it's practically impossible to figure out such answers. It's not because astrology is deficient, nor is it necessarily because the astrologer is deficient, it's because reality is what it is - extremely flexible and resilient.

Reality is a substance that changes when you touch it. We touch reality with our will, and it responds to that touch by morphing to facilitate the shape of our will, to the extent that we merit as a result of our cooperation with other beings who interact with the same reality.

In this fluid, flexible reality, how can an astrologer possibly know what happened to you on March 26, 1994 except by some divinely inspired guess? A divinely inspired guess is certainly wonderful, but it's not astrology, nor is it consistently reliable. There are dozens if not hundreds of things that *could have* happened to you on March 26, 1994 as a result of your destiny. Which one of those many possibilities came to pass depends on things that do not entirely fall within the purview of an astrological calculation, because they are determined by the interaction of your will with the substance of reality in the immediate past and the present.

A.C. Bhaktivedānta Swāmī gave an analogy comparing fate to being on an airplane. If I'm on an airplane to Chicago you know almost certainly that I will wind up in Chicago, but you don't know what seat I'll be in, if it will be bumpy, if I will be in the toilet when the "fasten seat-belts" sign goes on, etc. If you think about it, this analogy demonstrates that the consequential information is very easy to ascertain; while the stuff of much less consequence is not easy to foretell at all.

If we ask consequential questions we will easily get accurate and helpful answers. If we are obsessed with trying to control minor details of our immediate circumstances and try to use astrology as some metaphysical advantage to outsmart the universe, we will just chase our own tails from house to house in the horoscope, unable to see that we are going in circles due to the density of the fog of irrelevance.

Divination and Divinity

Astrology is a form of divination. *Divination* is the attempt to understand past, present and future. The word *divine* is pretty conspicuous as the root of the word *divination*. Knowledge is divine, and divination is the attempt to be godlike by gaining better knowledge of the divine plans of destiny.

The more intimately and deeply we are in touch with the divine, the less of a struggle it is to do divination effectively. Therefore, whether we want to be astrologers or want to be guided by astrologers, the first and foremost requisite for success is to *deepen our connection to the divine*.

I've found that it is relatively easy for spiritually deep people to do divination successfully, even without aid from astrology, palmistry or any other tool. Conversely, it is quite difficult for spiritually shallow people to divine accurately, even with all the methodology in the world. Of course, "spiritual depth" doesn't refer to stereotypical piety, religious affiliation, and so on. It refers to intimate inner contact with the divine, which itself is in no way limited to stereotypical religious definitions.

The bottom line is, if we want to give or receive divination, we should deepen our connection to divinity.

Connecting to the Divine

Every culture has many valuable methods of linking to divinity, but India is obsessed with the topic. She therefore presents us dozens, if not hundreds or even thousands of ways to deepen our connection to the divine. The Sanskrit word for these paths is yoga, which literally means, "to connect."

Although there are hundreds of yoga-paths, they all have the same aim: to dissolve false-ego (a self-concept divorced from the divine) and crystallize divine-ego (a self-concept rooted in the divine).

To understand how these yogas work, lets start by understanding how they define "the divine." Taittirīya Upanishad (Ānanda.7) offers this definition:

रसो वै सः

raso vai saḥ

He is certainly the experience of topmost joy.

This is an incredibly deep concept that deserves a lot of reflection. The most perfect and essential form of joy is love. Yet, love cannot be experienced in absolute solitude! Therefore, the divine, although singular and unified, must contain plurality.

As we previously learned, Vedānta explains the "The One shall be Many," expanding into countless divine beings – including you and I – to amplify and increase the infinite joy inherent in its being. If you consider this carefully, you'll get a sense for the most powerful and natural way to connect to divinity: by amplifying the bliss inherent in The One. The paths of yoga teaches, each in its own unique way, how to harmoniously receive, amplify, and return the current of ecstatic love effusing brilliantly and forcefully from the divine.

Currently we are in a condition of false-ego, which divorces us from this flow of joy and compels us to try and generate our own flow. False-ego sees itself not a planet orbiting the sun, but the sun orbited by planets. False-ego rejoices not in giving love to a divine center, but in the hopes of *being* the center around which everyone and everything else should be willing to revolve. This attitude has to dissolve before we can truly establish a deep, vivid and living connection to the divine.

There are so many religions and yoga-paths because there are so many different kinds of people. Each path is tailored towards the needs of different cultures and different groups of people. In the end, each *individual* has their own unique path. Each path is like a medicine. A pharmacy has so many medicines because there are so many different kinds of people with so many different illnesses. Health is the singular goal of all treatment, but each patient achieves health in different ways.

The hundreds of yoga-paths fall into three basic categories: Those that work by action, those that work by thought, and those that work by emotion.

Yogas of Action: Karma-Yoga

This very practical category of yoga deepens our connection to the divine by making our actions less self-centered. Two principles are essential to all varieties of *karma-yoga*: (1) responsibility, and (2) charity.

Responsibility means doing what you need to do before doing what you simply want to do. Recreation and relaxation is fine, but we must ensure that our responsibilities to others are taken care of *first*. Soon we find that enjoyment comes more powerfully from this than from seeking our own private ambitions and recreations. Consistent and carefully responsible action slackens our selfishness and thus erodes the main obstacle to communion with the divine.

Charity means giving your money, time, energy, and attention to those who need it, without expecting something in return. It's not easy to do this, because we need our resources to accomplish our personal desires. But this is exactly why regularly giving a portion of our resources to others is a powerful method of decreasing the selfish ego.

Yogas of Thought: Jñāna-Yoga

Yogas in this category work by using the intellect to identify and crush selfishness, resulting in stoic detachment from objects of pleasure and displeasure.

Look at things in the world and ask, "Is this me? Is this essential to me?" If we analyze anything carefully we'll come to conclusions like, "This thing is not me, for I am conscious of it from a separate vantage point. This thing is not essential to me, because it exists outside me and I can exist independently of it."

This kind of thinking invokes natural detachment from external things, which reduces our greeds, and thus weakens our selfishness.

It's not feasible to fully practice the yogas of knowledge without first making significant progress in the yogas of action, because unless one's ego is already somewhat purified it will bend and filter our knowledge to serve its own agenda. So the consistent recommendation is to practice *karma-yoga* while we are young and working, and transition to *jñāna-yoga* when we are older and retired. Nonetheless we can, and should, *begin* to explore the yogas of thought at any time. We don't have to be a total philosopher or scientist to benefit from their basic principles.

Yogas of Emotion: Bhakti-Yoga

Yogas in this category use the emotions to establish a loving relationship to the divine. This category is uniquely important for a few reasons.

- What we are really after in the first place is happiness, which comes from love. So naturally, the yogas of emotion and love are the most relevant.

- We use thoughts to plan our actions. This shows that thoughts control actions. But our emotions inspire and can easily overrule our thoughts, showing that emotion controls both thought and action. Accordingly, yogas of thought are more powerful than those of action, but yogas of emotion are the most powerful of all.

- Yogas of action and thought can dissolve the false-ego, but on their own they don't directly establish the divine ego (which by nature involves a loving connection to the divine).

That's why *karma* and *jñāna* (yogas of action and thought) are never prescribed in isolation. They are always infused with some amount of *bhakti* (the yoga of emotion). The yogas are inter-supportive. They do not compete with or contradict one another.

Bhakti is the center of the unit because nothing is more powerful and compelling than emotion. *Karma* and *jñāna* support and facilitate that center with responsibility, charity, and deep knowledge.

Bhakti-yoga directly focuses on becoming instrumental in the divine bliss shared between The One and The Many. It addresses The One with personal intimacy, using romantic names like Krishna (The All-Attractive), Govinda (The All-Delighting), Rāma (The All-Enjoying), and Hari (The Thief [of Hearts]).

The main way to practice *bhakti,* the yoga of love, is by hearing about Krishna, the object of love. The poems of The Beautiful Tales of the All-Attractive (Śrīmad Bhāgavata Purāṇa) are particularly important to hear and discuss.

This process of hearing about and discussing the beloved is called *kīrtan*. It becomes especially powerful *("saṁ-kīrtan")* when accompanied by music and done in the company of persons immersed in divine love. A specific *mantra* of divine names is particularly lauded for *saṅkīrtana*:

हरे कृष्ण हरे कृष्ण कृष्ण कृष्ण हरे हरे ।
हरे राम हरे राम राम राम हरे हरे ॥

Hare Krishna, Hare Krishna,
Krishna Krishna, Hare Hare
Hare Rāma, Hare Rāma,
Rāma Rāma, Hare Hare

If we avail ourselves of the relevant principles of *karma* and *jñāna yoga* as integral supports for *bhakti yoga* we will very quickly feel - in a real, tangible way - more intimately and deeply rooted in the divine. The vast improvement in our access to the wisdom of divination will be merely a curiosity compared to the treasures that will blossom in our lives.

About the Author

Born in Bay Shore, New York on July 27th, 1970 at 19:38, Vic DiCara was fascinated with astronomy as a young child. He became a hardcore-punk guitarist and songwriter in his late teens, and soon thereafter became deeply involved in the International Society for Krishna Consciousness, living for roughly 8 years in temples - studying elaborately and embarking on months of extended pilgrimages to the holy places of India. He was initiated into the *Gaudīya-sampradaya* and received the name Vraja Kishor dās, along with the brahminical thread as a symbol of his dedication to study. He studied sacred Sanskrit texts extensively under his guru, wrote prolifically to a large international audience, and was the founding headmaster of the first branch of the Vrindavana Institute for Higher Education in the Western world. At 28 he married and was blessed with a beautiful family. He began practicing astrology about a decade later and, thanks to his thorough spiritual background and familiarity with Sanskrit, quickly became recognized as an important exponent of the ancient science.

He currently lives in Japan, where he practices *bhakti-yoga,* gives astrological readings, and translates sacred *bhakti* texts into English. He and can be reached through his websites, VicDicara.com (for astrology) and VrajaKishor.com (for *bhakti*).

Other Books by the Author

27 Stars, 27 Gods

An unparalleled explanation of the deities in the 27 fixed stars *(nakṣatra)* of Indian ("Vedic") astrology, and the symbolic meaning they impart to the stars they empower.

A Simple Gītā

India's most essential spiritual text in an extremely enjoyable, compact, clear and straightforward format.

Beautiful Tales of the All-Attractive

Dramatic translation of the essential poetry of the yoga of love *(Śrīmad Bhāgavata Purāṇa)*, Canto One.

Creating the Creator

Śrīmad Bhāgavata Purāṇa, Canto Two: Telling the evolution of the universe and creation of the universe's creator, Brahmā.

Varāha, Vidura, and Kapila

Śrīmad Bhāgavata Purāṇa, Canto Three: Vidura hears the amazing tale of Viṣṇu's incarnation as a wild board, and Kapila explains the spiritual science called *saṅkhya.*

To Dance in the Downpour of Devotion

A clear presentation of *Mādhurya-kadambinī,* an incalculably valuable guidebook to the practice of *bhakti-yoga.*

Made in United States
Troutdale, OR
04/25/2024

19439094R10054